This book is dedicated to my wife Rama, my love, rock, and business partner.

Table of Contents

Prelude

Chapter 1--Become Debt Free

Chapter 2--Save Raises

Chapter 3--One-to-Two Technologies Behind

Chapter 4--Work Hard Play Hard

Chapter 5--Private Schools and Out-of-State Colleges

Chapter 6--Leased Cars and Car Loans

Chapter 7--Financial Calculators

Chapter 8--Big House ≠ Medium and Small House

Chapter 9--Don't Waste Money

Chapter 10--You Can't Take It With You

Chapter 11--Don't Need a Million Dollars

Chapter 12--Charity and Cheerful Giving

Conclusion

Prelude

Would you like to accomplish financial freedom without having to win the lottery or inherit money? Would you like to pay your household bills in full when they come each month? Would you like the freedom and autonomy to pay your expenses in full with cash or with credit cards to capitalize on rewards. Would you like to pre-fund your vacations in full prior to departure? Would you like to cheerfully give to others without it affecting you financially? Would you like to pay your monthly bills and have money left over to invest? Would you like to generate passive income from income other people earn? If your answer to any of those questions are yes, then this is the book you can't afford not to read. Anyone can achieve all of the financial milestones mentioned, regardless of income if you apply the money secrets hiring in plain sight. I decided to write this book to be a roadmap for people who didn't inherit money to obtain financial freedom, no matter your income. I know the strategies in this book work, because I used them to become successful and want to share them with as many people as possible.

It is apparent that we are living in tough financial times. We are dealing with a recession, monkeypox public health emergency, remnants of the multi-year coronavirus pandemic, and record inflation, to name a few. We also have to be honest that income level doesn't determine if you will be financial free or not. I know for a fact that individuals with high incomes borrow against their employer retirement plans and retirement accounts for various reasons. Therefore, you cannot hide behind your salary and act like you are immune to tough financial times. Generally, the more money you make, the more you spend on your bills. For example, people are more likely to spend up to their full affordability on a house rather than half their affordability. There are a plethora of certified financial planners, books, and information on the internet that are easily available for anyone to obtain financial freedom. Well, are they working? I agree the information is available; however, it seems that only a small portion of the population is benefiting.

I know by now you are wondering what's so different from this book and the many others available. The answer is, if you aren't where you want to be financially, you can't afford not to read this book. I'm certain this is the book the middle and low-income classes worldwide need to become financially fit. You can begin putting the strategies in this book in place immediately and you will see results. I know this is true, because the strategies have brought me success and I have direct experience with being both middle and low-income. In addition, this book is short, to the point, and easy to read. The middle and low-income classes are the backbone of the economy and this book can get the economy back on track. I expect some people to disagree with one or more of the strategies discussed in this book. However, I challenge you to read the entire book, then self-reflect on your life. Only you can decide if this is worth a try. However, I assure you that these strategies have produced real success in our lives. So much success, that at times it's hard to relate to others and their situations. For example, there is a big difference in being able to drive a $100,000 car and purchase five bitcoins. The bitcoin investment can quadruple your money, while the car will surely depreciate. Be warned, the strategies in this book involve hard work and discipline. However, don't let hard work scare you. Because when it's all said and done, you don't want to be caught starting your conversations with I would have, could have, or should have done something different.

Chapter 1

Become Debt Free

This is the first chapter, because I believe this is the foundation. It is virtually impossible to improve your financial picture until you wall-off and contain your bad debt. By far, the most common is credit card debt. In this section, I will briefly provide some techniques on becoming debt free. The first thing you have to realize is, you can only control so much in life and a number of things will negatively affect you no matter how prepared you are. For example, on average you will face at least two unexpected situations annually that require more money that's within your monthly budget to address (e.g., replace vehicle tires, replace house roof, inclement weather damage, etc.). In order to properly address these issues, you must have your monthly budget under control and an emergency fund established. With that said, it's important to trim the fat in your lifestyle and budget to prepare you for times of scarcity.

Start with easy areas, such as services and subscriptions that are duplicative or you rarely use. That way, when times of scarcity arrive (e.g., layoff or large medical expense), only minor lifestyle changes are needed, if any. The money left over after trimming the fat should be applied to your credit card debt, starting with the highest interest rate. If you have a large credit card balance, I recommend paying the minimum balance from your primary checking account and establishing a direct deposit savings account at another financial institution that is out-of-sight, in order to build-up a sufficient lump sum. Then, pay-off the large credit card balance once you have enough in your lump sum. I know from experience that it's extremely hard to pay-off a large credit card balance using the money in an account that you are balancing monthly bills, minimal payments, and expenses. After the credit card balance is paid, you will have to decide whether to close the account, shred the credit card, or both. Now, down to the techniques I promised you. There are so many ways to save money to pay-off debt and many of them you probably know of or are doing. Below is a list that applies to virtually any household.

- Before going grocery shopping, monitor sales and clip printed and digital coupons.
- Try to limit grocery store shopping to twice or three times a month.
- Cook large meals that you can eat for a few days.
- Reduce car insurance to liability on old, paid-off vehicles.
- Downsize to a one or two vehicle household for as long as you can.
- Bring your lunch to work as much as possible.
- Refrain from buying multiple items that perform the same functions, such as multiple watches or paying for a gym membership when you have exercise equipment at home.
- Wait for electronics to go on sale; trust me they will.
- For big purchases, such as furniture and large appliances, look for 12-to-18-month interest free financing options and pay them off on-time.
- Conduct research for a generous rewards credit card to charge items you both need and can afford and let the rewards pile up. Then, redeem them for items you want, even airplane tickets.

- Don't be too proud to shop at thrift stores. Some clothes still have new tags on them. You will be shocked to see who shops at thrift stores, people with multiple investment properties.
- Never send your entire paycheck to a single bank account. Establish a checking account (joint checking for couples) for all household bills. Establish a separate direct deposit account for spending money and another account for savings.
- Look for any available discounted tickets (military, senior, child, membership, etc.) for any entertainment venue (movies, skating, concerts, sports games, shows, etc.).
- Shop for local used cars in good condition and pay them off in four years or less.
- Try to maintain a saving/investing amount that exceeds your vehicle's odometer number. In other words, does the amount you have saved exceed the number on your vehicle's odometer?

By utilizing those techniques, you should be able to trim the fat in your budget, which will enable you to get out of debt, save an emergency fund and invest in your goals and dreams.

Chapter 2

Save Raises

Finding ways to save your money is essential to gaining financial freedom. Although investing plays a crucial role as well, you first need a foundation. In order to have a foundation, you must spend less money than you earn. Please listen closely to this. Material things that don't pay you passive income, only gets you bragging rights. At the end of the day, you are stuck paying the bill, not the people you are trying to impress. If you have a monthly payment on material things such as a vehicle or boat and it's beyond your means, it can be taken away from you along with the money you put into it. Therefore, it's imperative that you make purchases that you can afford and have an emergency fund that covers at least a few months of expenses. A good strategy to build your financial foundation is to save a portion or all of your raises (increase in hourly pay) and bonuses. The goal is to have the savings going to a place that is out-of-sight. Prior to the raise you didn't have the additional money, so you don't have to be in a hurry to spend it.

I'm not saying that you shouldn't upgrade your lifestyle as you make more money. This is expected. However, you shouldn't tailor your bills to match your total income. Just because you make twice as much as you made 10 years ago, doesn't mean you should spend twice as much in bills. Remember, as you make more money, you generally get taxed at a higher rate. Committing most or all your monthly income to bills can create a disaster. This is a problem because, you are assuming everything will always be okay and trials will not come. Let's get real, who knows when a family member will get sick, have a serious accident, or pass away. Let's say you have a household monthly income of $10,000 per month, mortgage on your house, a couple of cars loans, and kids. If an emergency occurred and one parent was unable to work for an extended period, would your family be able to live off 5 to 6 thousand dollars a month? In most cases the answer is no, because household bills tend to equal income.

If you have a one income household, can you pay your bills if your salary was reduced by one-third for an extended period? This is why it's so important to have an emergency fund and I recommend saving a portion or all of your future raises and bonuses. Obviously, I'm assuming that you don't have credit card debt, which would take precedence. It wouldn't make sense to save money making 2% interest and continue to pay the minimum balance of credit card debt at 17%. The objective is to consistently live below your means and the money you save over the years will quickly grow and will be there when you need it. You need to first establish an emergency fund, before worrying about investing. Good places to start saving are money market accounts and certificates of deposits (CDs) at both FDIC insured banks and credit unions. You shouldn't commit all your savings to a long-term CD, just in case an unexpectant expense occurs.

If you receive a raise, I recommend you set-up a saving or checking account, preferably at a separate bank or credit union from your primary one. You will be surprised how much the balance can be in as little as six to nine months, if you don't touch it. You should continue to save your money until you have a balance of at least $10,000. Then, you can transfer the majority of that money into a one- or two-year CD, which will earn you interest monthly. Each year, continue to save raises and disposable income to a separate account. You don't have to set-up one additional account, you can do multiple (savings, checking, money market accounts, and CDs) across many financial institutions. After your emergency fund is established and you are fully funding your retirement accounts, you can expand to saving at investment institutions (mutual funds, education savings accounts, exchange-traded funds, individual stocks, etc.). However, the focus of this book is establishing a strong foundation and not investing.

Since you now have money saved, you can pay for your vacations and material things with cash, instead of making monthly payments. Once you have at least $20,000 in your CD, you can roll it over for three to five years to get a higher interest rate. Remember, never get so aggressive and place all your liquid savings into a CD, because you never know when you will need to address an emergency. Now that you've been consistently saving for three to five years, you probably have paid-off your car. Guess what you are going to do with the extra $400 to $600 dollars a month? You guessed right, send the extra money (pay yourself first) to the one or more accounts you established at various financial institutions. If you saved the money that was previously going to a car loan for five years, you would have saved approximately $36,000. Now, imagine being ready to go get your next car loan with $36,000 and all the other money you have across various financial institutions.

The goal is to minimize your resource dependency from your job in higher increments, with each passing year. This will ultimately give you the freedom of your time and the ability to earn money doing work that aligns to your passions. If you were able to completely replace your income you make at work, what would you want to do? This strategy is doable for anyone and any income level. It just takes discipline. It's important that you set-up multiple accounts, so you don't look at all your money on a day-to-day basis. Continue these steps and you will be well on your way to paying off your bills, paying cash for purchases, and establishing your emergency fund. Remember the emergency fund is mandatory and you should make sure you have it before investing aggressively. I will briefly touch on different investing options later in this book.

Chapter 3

One-to-Two Technologies Behind

I'm not suggesting that you buy inferior or the cheapest technology you can find. What I'm saying is, it's futile to consistently stay on top with the latest technology and become financially fit at the same time. It's simply unrealistic. As soon as the latest and greatest product is released, research and design is being done to create something better and faster. I'm not saying to never make purchases. If you can afford it, there's nothing wrong with purchasing top-of-the-line products when you need it, not just because they are new. You should get your money's worth out of the products before you replace them. Getting your money's worth, may result in you being one-to-two technologies behind before you replace your products. After you make your technology decisions, pay them off, and enjoy them without payments for a while. For example, the newest technology probably has two additional features than the one you own. Why buy the new one, if you haven't paid off the one you have. Also, try not to use the justification that you need to give your current product to your child, which provides you the opportunity to get the product you really want. Although this may be the case sometimes, it usually isn't. A good strategy to use for buying technology products is to look for free upgrades, promotions, and holiday deals. You should constantly monitor deals that are available and when they fit the things you need, you should be able to pay for them in cash or reward points, if you follow the steps in Chapters 1 and 2.

I hardly ever get top-of-the-line products when they are first released, because I want to get them on sale later. It's like a game for me. My goal is to save 30 to 50 percent off the original price. For many years, the speed of technology changes has continued to accelerate. Therefore, trust your reasons for purchasing your electronics and hold on to them. No matter what you buy, it won't be the top-of-the-line for long. You must look at your financial picture and first determine how much you can spend. Then, apply that amount to the market and don't do it vice-versa. Once you do your research and make your purchase decision, stick with it and be happy. Trust me, you will be able to save a considerable amount over time, by getting your money's worth on purchases. Then, when the right time comes, trade-in, sell, or gift your old electronics to others. With so many electronic marketplaces available, it's easier than ever to sell used electronics, without doing a yard sale. Let's say your child wants the latest-and-greatest video game system and it costs $400. For that price, you will only get the console and one controller. However, it's likely that if you wait a year and a half, do your research, and catch a sale, you can get those contents plus two games and a second controller for $300. I know what you are thinking. That's a long time to wait to get the video game system when your child wants it now and I agree. However, these three things will remain true. First, it's best to buy products when you are financially ready and receive the best value for your money. Second, there will still be a lot of people playing the current video game system your child has. Lastly, there will still be a lot of people playing the new system when your child finally gets it.

Chapter 4

Work Hard Play Hard

I believe there is a lot of truth in William Newnham's phrase, "work hard play hard." You can apply this to many different areas of your life. Literally any significant achievement in life takes time, commitment, investment, and/or discipline. The examples I will briefly discuss in this chapter are career, education, car, and family. It's obvious that it takes hard work, grace, and opportunities to reach your career goals. No one owes you anything and you will have to go out and prove your commitment and value to your organization or customers. This is referred to as "paying your dues." I know some people receive promotions through "hook-ups" and making their co-workers look bad; however, the truth will eventually come out. We've all had bosses that didn't know much about their job and needed to be trained by their staff. But for most of the workforce, years and years of consistent hard work is needed to move up in your career and become successful.

The same applies to professional entertainers and athletes. Even though many people feel that these individuals don't deserve their high salaries, you cannot deny that they are experts in their field and have been training non-stop for the majority of their lives. The same concept can be applied to obtaining a college degree. Although degrees require a great deal of time, discipline and money; they can put you in a position to be successful in the workforce. The next example that requires discipline is purchasing a car. Later in this book, I will discuss how you should approach car buying, but for now I will point out the fact that buying and paying-off a car takes hard work. In order to obtain the car loan, you need a good credit score. I'm certain that when you are paying a car loan, you will take care of the car and avoid unnecessary risks. On the other hand, when a car is given as a gift, the same type of pride and emotional connection will not be present. You will also be more likely to let friends borrow and race the car, simply because your hard-earned money wasn't spent to purchase it.

The last example is family. We all know that family is one of the most important parts of our lives. Family is the reason why most people go to work, get a second job, go back to school, go without sleep, and miss meals. Although family can pull you in multiple directions, you must adapt and overcome, because failure is not an option. We are willing to be creative and humble ourselves to take care of our families. We also know that spending quality time and maintaining healthy relationships with family is hard work. Becoming financially fit takes a similar type of discipline as in the examples I mentioned. It's simple, if you quit prematurely, you won't reach your potential. This brings me to my last point of this chapter. Be cautious of get rich quick schemes.

If you believe something is too good to be true; it likely is. If an opportunity doesn't include hard work, innovation, and/or discipline, it's not worth your time. It sounds good to exert minimal effort and magically other people make you a lot of money; however, it almost never happens that way. If you are not willing to do the work, don't expect to reap the benefits. Remember, no one owes you anything nor do they care if you become successful. Therefore, you must make the decision to do whatever is necessary to become financially fit. Once you have your foundation (emergency fund) in place, you can then play hard. When I say play hard, I mean investing, vacationing, being a blessing to others, and pursuing your interests. Your journey doesn't have to be pretty or glamorous, you just have to get there. Once you get there, you won't have to start over, unless you forget what got you there in the first place.

Chapter 5

Private Schools and Out-of-State Colleges

Some people may disagree with me on this topic, but just hear me out. Private schools cost on average $12,000 per year, which include elementary, middle, and secondary schools. I'm also aware that many private schools have scholarship and grant programs. However, if your household income is less than the top 10% of the United States, which is approximately $200,000, you should not be paying for private schools. I understand that the student-to-teacher ratio is lower and some have a more comprehensive academic program than public schools; however, you should look into other options if you can't afford private schools. This situation is similar to purchasing a vehicle. Everyone is not going to be able to buy the full-size, fully loaded luxury car. That's why there are variations in vehicle sizes and packages. Just as you can find a reliable vehicle to get you from one place to another, you can find a desirable area with good public schools.

A good friend told me that it makes sense to pay a little more and buy a house in a good school district than to buy a better house in a less desirable school district. I'm sure you can find a house in a good school district, where the mortgage is less than paying an additional $12,000 annually per child for K-12 education. The fact that we are in a recession should be an indicator that the economy is not going to always perform well. That's why it's important to not spend all your money during times of plenty, because you don't know when times of scarcity will occur and for how long. Your significant other may get sick or lose their job at any point and there goes your budget. My recommendation is to leave private schools to the individuals who can comfortably afford it and look to rent or buy a residence in an area with good public schools. Believe me, they are out there. If you buy a house, you also must consider that approximately 40 to 50 percent of your annual property taxes are allocated to funding the public school system. Therefore, why would you want to pay twice for your child's education? Regardless of your income, you should be fully funding your retirements accounts and taking advantage of your employer's 401(k)/403(b) match before paying for private schools.

The next section of this chapter pertains to out-of-state colleges. The same concept I discussed earlier with private schools apply to out-of-state colleges. Again, why pay taxes in one state and pay out-of-state tuition in another. I understand the argument that a particular school may have a renowned program, such as marine biology or petroleum engineering; however, I believe most academic programs are provided at local or state universities. You don't have to go to an Ivy League university to get a law degree or go to an out-of-state college to obtain a history degree. You can have a successful career by getting your degree at a university near your home or even online as a non-traditional student. If you pay taxes in one state, why would you pay an additional $12,000 or more per year to send your young adult child to another state to attend a college, which could be done cheaper and closer to home? I don't recommend buying anything as a status symbol. Your purchases should be aligned to your financial plan, goals, and budget. Let's be honest, is it worth sending your child away to rack up $100,000 in student loans, just so they can come right back home to live with you again?

I will take it a step further. Why would you send your child to a local university and pay for room and board? While this is a less expensive alternative to sending your child to an out-of-state college, you are still paying twice for lodging. Why not allow your child to continue to stay at home and save money. I know it won't make your child happy; however, it will put you in a better position to retire and not be a burden to your child later in life. Remember, you are going to want to retire at some point. If your child attends a local university, you will likely be paying for their car, gas, and insurance. Why also pay for an apartment? Unless your child earns a scholarship, my recommendation is to send your child to a community college for the first two years. The first two years of college comprise of general classes that can be taken at a community college for half or sometimes a fourth of the cost at a university. Again, why spend more when your child can get an education at a local accredited educational institution. In addition, some community colleges have articulation agreements with four-year academic institutions, which allow a seamless transfer process. Your child might not like it; however, in most cases they're not paying for it. I recommend not paying for private schools or out-of-state colleges unless your household income is in excess of $200,000 and you can afford to also fully fund your retirement accounts.

Chapter 6

Leased Cars and Car Loans

If there is one place I know money can be saved, it's in this category. The drastic increase in vehicle costs have contributed to consumers being overcome by vehicle debt. It has gotten so bad that it seems some people care more about their vehicles than where they live. We must go back to the basics. Just like the primary function of cell phones is to communicate, the purpose of vehicles is to get us from one place to another safely and reliably. I understand that as our income rises, we should steadily upgrade our vehicles. However, we have to first define our vehicle needs instead of letting society do it. It's fine to just have one vehicle, if that fits your needs. Additionally, you aren't required to have a large SUV, just because you have a family. Essentially, you need to make the decision on what vehicle is best for your family, regardless of what anyone else thinks. Unless someone decides to buy you a vehicle, you need to be the person who makes the final decision and not peers or friends.

Let's first discuss leased cars. I acknowledge there are situations where leasing a car makes sense. A good example would be leasing a car for the tax deductions/write-offs for your business. The Internal Revenue Service (IRS) permits 100% of car lease payments as eligible vehicle deductions. I also acknowledge that there are some really attractive lease rates available for fully-loaded and luxury cars. However, don't decide to lease a car without determining the true cost of the lease (acquisition fee, down payment, security deposit, disposition fee, etc.) and comparing the cost of purchasing a vehicle. You must also consider the mileage restrictions and number of years of the vehicle lease. The total amount of money spent on leasing a vehicle can be shocking, especially if you do back-to-back leases. You can easily spend $17,500 or more over a three-year vehicle lease. Unfortunately, at the end of the contract, you won't be able to trade-in or sell the leased vehicle for money nor can you continue to drive the car.

Let's assume you have a vehicle you purchased new nine years ago and it has less than 162,000 miles. You paid it off in four years and have been driving it for five years with no car payment. If you saved the monthly car payment that you didn't have to pay for the last five years, you would be able to purchase your next car outright in cash and would have a trade-in! If you are leasing a vehicle you can't afford to buy to impress others, you should finish your contract and buy a car that fits your budget and needs. Also, do not lease a car, because it's your dream car. If you save and make the right financial decisions, you may be able to afford and own your dream car one day.

Now, let's discuss car loans. Essentially, any fully-loaded new vehicle will cost at least $30,000 these days. Also, gone are the days of the standard vehicle loan being 60 months. Now, car sellers are creative to find ways to make expensive cars seem affordable, by extending the car loan to 84 months. It's important that you stay within your price range even if it means you must buy a used car. As time goes by, you will be able to progressively afford more expensive cars. It's important that you do not take on more vehicle debt that you can handle for a couple of reasons. The first reason is obvious. If you buy a car that is too expensive, you run the risk of not being able to afford it and it can negatively affect your credit. Your credit score can affect you in many different ways. Bad credit can result in higher insurance premiums and difficulty in obtaining housing, a job, and household furnishings. This is a very stressful position to be in. It's not fun to have to determine which bills you will or will not pay.

The second reason is, if you buy a car that you can't afford, you will still likely make your next car bigger and better. There is no way that you are going to level down from a luxury to a standard vehicle, unless you experience an extreme financial set-back. For example, if you purchase a luxury vehicle, your next car is likely not going to be a standard vehicle, unless you are purchasing it for your child. For this same reason, I caution parents to not start their kids off with expensive vehicles. As novice drivers, your kids will get into accidents, street races, and will let their friends and significant others drive the cars you give them. If you give a 16-year-old a luxury or sports car as a first vehicle, he or she will not be mature enough to take care of it like a mature adult. Unless you can truly afford it, it's best to not purchase a luxury vehicle first. Instead, start somewhere in the middle, so that you will have room to upgrade as your income grows.

I have a car challenge for you that will enable you to save a significant amount of money over time. The challenge is to only buy vehicles that you can afford to pay-off in four years. Get a five-year (60 month) car loan; however, pay a little extra each month and pay it off early. This challenge goes for both new and used cars. This will enable you to save money on interest and free you up to save or pay down other debt starting the fifth year of your vehicle loan. Depending on how much you drive your vehicle, you should be able to keep it for seven to nine years. Many employers are now allowing employees to work at home remotely or telework under a hybrid schedule, enabling many individuals to extend the life of their vehicles. If you can pay your vehicle off in four years and can go without a car payment for three to four years, you can save between 14 to 20 thousand dollars between car loans. If you are unable to pay-off your car in four years, don't be discouraged. Make this your goal that you work towards. Remember, you still have to keep up with your vehicle's preventative maintenance to preserve it as long as possible. Implementing this challenge can literally save you thousands over time. If not, you will continue to pay a vehicle loan or lease every year and wonder where your hard-earned money is going.

Chapter 7

Financial Calculators

There is a plethora of financial calculators available that can help people gain insights on how much debt they can afford for cars, boats, and houses, as well as how much they can save over time at various interest rates of return. They are located on a variety of websites all over the internet. Although they are a good tool to be used as a guide or benchmark, they should be used as a starting point and not to make your final decision. You and your family should make the final decision on what you can afford, such as your total percentage of income for housing. A financial calculator may indicate that you can afford to spend 28% of your monthly income on housing. However, you are free to change it to 25%, if that aligns to your budget and goals.

It's important to make sure you are honest when using financial calculators. Don't omit bills or loans, because you expect to pay them off in the future. An unforeseen issue can prevent you from paying off your debt as planned. You should run accurate calculations so that they reflect your accurate financial picture. You may find out that making a purchase will result in your expenses exceeding your income or the increase from your promotion. Another reason why you shouldn't make decisions solely based on financial calculators is, there will be indirect costs associated with each individual purchase and budget. Many times, we only focus on the direct costs and not the indirect costs. For example, if you base your affordability for a mortgage on just the principal and interest payment, it will be difficult to afford the utilities, association fees, insurance, taxes, and cleaning/lawn services.

If you buy a large house, not only will it be expensive to heat and cool it, every expense that the house generates will be more than your previous costs. Therefore, it's important that you know the direct and indirect costs of a big house before you buy it. This will help you determine if you can afford it and if it makes sense for you and your family. If you have a small household, why would you want to heat, cool, clean, and dust a big empty house that you may not get the opportunity to enjoy. There are other indirect costs associated with a house as well. You also have to furnish it, both inside and outside. This includes beds, dressers, furniture, patio/deck equipment, and more. Furnishing a house can easily cost or exceed $30,000. Therefore, it's advantageous to have those costs already saved or have a plan to purchase the items over time or with no interest financing, instead of charging thousands of dollars of debt you can't afford.

Chapter 8

Big House ≠ Medium and Small House

Do you think purchasing a big house is equal to or greater than a medium and small house? In most cases, it's not. However, the answer depends on your overall financial picture. Your overall financial picture includes how much money you earn, how much you spend on bills and liabilities, the amount you have available to invest, and whether you own rental property. There was a time when I felt confident that it was better to have a large house over two smaller ones. However, I will explain why I now believe it's better to have two smaller ones. As I mentioned in the previous chapter, a house involves numerous direct and indirect costs. The larger the house, the larger the costs. First, having a big house will not ensure your happiness. It's more important to buy a house you can afford, in a good neighborhood and close proximity to desirable schools. It's better to buy a medium size house in a good location rather than a large house in an undesirable area.

Also, in today's society, it is difficult to enjoy a large house, unless you are wealthy, because our lives are simply too busy. First, you will spend the majority of your time at work and commuting, which will hinder your ability to clean your home. When you are at home, you will be busy preparing meals, spending time with family and close friends, winding down, and sleeping. So, you have to ask yourself, do you really have a lot of time to enjoy a big house? You may find yourself working 50-to-60-hour weeks to pay the bills and paying others to run your errands, clean your house, and maintain your yard. In this situation, your house will only consume money rather than provide you money. Eventually, you will become frustrated with having little disposable income, despite earning a good income.

Now, let's look at having a medium and small size house. Be advised that this scenario will only work if you can afford both houses. Depending on your financial situation, you can buy both at one time or one at a time. The concept is to live in one of the houses and rent the other one. Choose the house you will live in based on your household size and needs and investment strategy. Let's discuss what these homes should look like. If all possible, I recommend you invest in three-bedroom townhomes and single family homes to maximize your rental market and appeal to families. If you don't have at least three bedrooms, it could be too small to generate the desired amount of monthly rent. You want your rentals to be marketable to as many people as possible. Your challenge will be to pay all or the majority of both mortgages with your monthly income and save as much as you can in rent payments. If you do this faithfully, your savings will grow at a fast rate.

For example, if you receive $1500 monthly in rental income, that's $18,000 a year. I understand that as a landlord, you may have to cover expenses, such as the mortgage, utilities, homeowners' association dues, and escrow; however, the more money you can save after expenses the better. Being a homeowner and landlord, you will have the potential to tap into increased tax incentives to include depreciation, operating expenses, and repairs. This is in addition to the rental income and appreciation growth of the rental property. Therefore, if you are able to find two properties that you can afford in a desirable location, I recommend considering it.

Would you rather have a big house that looks good or be in a situation where you can supplement your savings with money you didn't work for and build wealth? This seems to be a no-brainer for me. As your income and equity increases, you can slowly acquire more rental properties. Be cautious not to buy more properties than you can handle in an attempt to speed up the process. Remember, this will only work if you have the monthly income to cover all mortgages and expenses, especially when your rental property is vacant. You never want to put yourself in a situation where you have more money going out than you do coming in. As time goes on, your rental properties will pay for themselves and help you purchase your big house, if you are patient. At that time, you will be generating income instead of only earning it.

Chapter 9

Don't Waste Money

The title of this chapter is self-explanatory. Some people have a lot of money, while others do not. If you are one of the fortunate people that have a lot of money, there is a difference in enjoying your money and wasting it. We all have seen examples of individuals who have wasted large sums of money on mansions, expensive luxury cars, and material possessions and have nothing to show for it several years later. These individuals include entertainers, professional athletes, and lottery winners. I will provide you an example of enjoying and wasting your money. Taking an around the world trip is an example of enjoying your money. This is an experience that you will cherish the rest of your life. You will have the opportunity to experience places and cultures for the first time that you read about online or in books. This experience will also provide you the opportunity to share and have meaningful conversations with family and friends on places abroad. Obviously, this trip will cost a lot of money, however, you can easily see the value.

On the other hand, purchasing 10 vehicles, because you can't think of anything else to buy or you want to impress others, is wasteful. You can only drive one vehicle at a time and will have to do maintenance on all of them whether you want to or not. You will experience the same type of happiness with a few fully loaded vehicles that you would if you purchased 10. It's expected that you will spend more money as you make more. What people don't realize is that wasting your money on things you don't need will not bring you happiness. In many cases, it will bring you grief and frustration, especially if you have to sell your material possessions for pennies on the dollar. Then, someone who can actually afford your possessions will gladly swoop in to get a steal of a deal. Do you really need more than a family vehicle, truck, and a sedan?

I also understand that you may need multiple vehicles if you have a large family. However, I have personally seen a family of five drivers share three vehicles. Even though this may seem unusual, this family had a plan and knew how to sacrifice. Oh, I forgot to mention that this family lived in a beautiful waterfront two story house in a gated community and owned a family business. If you ask me, they had their priorities in the right place. Instead of showing their wealth in their cars, they decided to put their wealth in their house and business. Also, the parents did not pay for private school for their kids; they sent them to public magnet schools. Magnet schools provides a public education that focuses on performing arts, science, and math for elementary, middle and high school students. If you have the option to send your kids to a magnet school, I highly recommend it.

There are a lot of things you can do with your money instead of wasting it. You can invest it in the stock market, buy a franchise, establish a profit or non-profit business, purchase an investment property, contribute to company and individual retirement accounts, or give to charity. All of these options will either grow your portfolio, bring you happiness, or provide you a sense of achievement, pride, and affiliation. As mentioned earlier, don't assume you will never go through hard times. You may feel that you are on top of the rock right now, but situations change, and life happens. People get sick, lose their job, divorce, or pass away with little notice. Therefore, your situation can be very different next year than this year. You need to be realistic with your affordability, prioritize your spending, and focus on your family. You should always be concerned with your family's needs rather than impressing others. Therefore, if you are doing the right things with your money, others will probably not notice you, unless they are in your inner circle. When you spend your hard-earned money on something, make sure you get your money's worth out of it. If you are unable to get your money's worth out of it, donate and bless someone else with it.

Chapter 10

You Can't Take It With You

In the last chapter, I discussed the importance of not wasting money. However, you shouldn't take it to the extreme and find yourself afraid to enjoy life and purchase the things you need. It's fine to have financial goals; however, you shouldn't be in love or greedy with money, because you can always make more of it. One day we will pass away and leave all our wealth here; however, that doesn't mean you should come up with a strategy to spend every dollar you earn. If this is your strategy, you will likely run out of money and regret your decision. I will briefly discuss three money practices that tend to lead to negative financial results. First, some people don't save for the future or consider that bad times will come. They just live for today and do not plan for the future. With so many luxuries and material items flashed in front of our eyes each day, some people have forgotten how to save and budget for purchases.

We are in a society that makes you believe that if you can afford the monthly payment, you are fine. This can get you into real trouble. Let's be honest, we all in some manner, live paycheck-to-paycheck. In other words, if we don't get paid from our employer or business, we would not be able to pay our bills, or would have to take money from our emergency fund. For that reason alone, it's important to save a portion of the money you earn. The goal is to get to the point where you are saving an amount that is comfortable for you every month. It doesn't have to be the same consistent amount, just make sure you save a portion. It's important to start saving each month, rather than waiting until you can set-aside a certain lump sum amount.

Let me give you a practical reason why you should save. The average working-class parents are away from home for 12 hours a day, between commuting, going back and forth to childcare, and being at work. It increases to 13 hours on the days they have to go to the grocery store. There are many times when they are extremely exhausted throughout the entire day. Given the situation I described, how dare we spend every penny of our hard-earned money each month. After all, we should put a value on our time it took to earn the money. Now think about your specific situation. Are you effectively saving your money or is there fat to be trimmed from your budget? It's up to you to make an accurate assessment and incorporate some or all of the topics covered in this book, if necessary.

As I said earlier, bad things happen in life, which can range from having to replace a tire to having a major medical emergency. When bad times occur, you want to be able to take the money out of your emergency fund and address it. If you are only living for today, it will be extremely difficult to address emergencies. The second money practice is you deserve to get whatever you want now. Before you go on a shopping spree, you need to find out how to make your money work for you (earn you money without working for it). It's a natural tendency to want the latest technology; however, you can only acquire so much if you want to build wealth. You will be okay financially if you get what you need and plan out your wants.

There have been many published studies on the profile and characteristics of a millionaire. There is a high likelihood that people that appear to have a lot of money, lack investable assets and own very little. Therefore, you may have the wrong idea of what a millionaire looks like. If you don't know what a millionaire looks like, chances are you do not know how they think and will not become one. There are many people that earn a high salary, possess a lot of material possessions, but are not millionaires. They may look like millionaires, but they maybe far from it. In fact, they may not even have an adequate emergency fund. You are probably wondering how can someone that earns a six-figure salary be far from becoming a millionaire. The reasons are lifestyle and status. People are pressured by the media, colleagues, and family to live a certain lifestyle based on their income and occupation.

My advice to you is to have confidence in yourself and not be influenced to do things for social acceptance. As I said earlier, you should make purchases that make sense for your budget and family. It's okay to enjoy material possessions and life, if you can afford it. You also must understand that there will always be someone that has more resources than you. However, that doesn't mean that they will be happier than you. Although I may feel I deserve a luxury car, that doesn't mean I'm entitled to it now if I haven't properly prepared myself to purchase it. Don't be in a rush to get expensive material possessions. Rather, get them when they fit easily within your budget. If you work hard for it, you will appreciate and take better care of it. Why should you care if someone gets a material possession before you? You will enjoy it the same when the time is right and you can afford it.

The third money practice is thinking I should spend all my money because I can't take it with me. While you cannot take it with you, you should consider leaving a legacy (money and property) to your family. Do you ever wonder why some families own multiple properties, businesses, or have the resources to run for public offices? It's called old money. The earlier you purchase a property or invest in a business venture that you can afford, the better off you and your family will be in the future. I'll give you an example. Let's assume you purchased a home 10 years ago for $300,000. Now, homes in your area are worth $400,000. By now, you have a great deal of equity in your house; encompassing the balance you have paid down on your loan and the increase in property value.

Now, let's contrast your situation with someone else who decides to buy a house in your neighborhood for $400,000. Even though that person has the resources to afford the house, he or she must also factor in the costs to make repairs and the indirect costs. You on the other hand, should be making considerably more income than you were 10 years ago and have the opportunity to grow your portfolio, by purchasing an investment property or investing your additional money. You are now on the path to not only paying off your first home, but also paying the mortgage down on an investment property with money earned from tenants, which will grow your net worth. Now, you are on your way to providing a better life for yourself and your children.

It would not be wise to cash in your home equity or sell your properties to spend all your money before you pass away. Why spend it all, when you don't know how long you will live or if you will become very ill. I agree that you should enjoy your money, however, I would not focus my energy on trying to spend everything I have before I pass away. If you do that, the next generation will have to start all over again just like you did. It's time to break the cycle. If you over-extend yourself financially, that will lead to additional stress. That stress can lead to high-blood pressure, stroke, insomnia, anxiety, and much more. Financial problems can restrict your ability to get healthcare, buy food or pay your bills, which could leave you homeless. Therefore, before you devise a plan to spend all your money before you pass-away, remember running out of money can be catastrophic.

Chapter 11

Don't Need a Million Dollars

In this chapter, I will explain how money isn't the center of all happiness. Money can buy many things, but not everything. Three major things money can't buy are time, love, and happiness. No matter how much money we accumulate, we all will surely die and leave it here. Therefore, it's in our best interest to live life to the fullest and cherish every moment you can with family and friends. As I stated in the last chapter, you should save your money and leave some to your next of kin. However, you should not let a love of money hinder you from enjoying life. After you work hard, don't forget to play hard. Always strive to be there for your family, especially your children.

Remember, material possessions will never take the place of quality time. This is a major problem families face across many socioeconomic groups. People are so busy trying to pay the bills and make a living, they are unable to spend quality time with their families. Take the time to mend relationships and show your family they are important to you before time is up. Remember, time stops for no one. By now, you have probably heard a hundred times that money can't buy you love. As long as you have money, you won't have a shortage of people at your side. The problem is, people will not truly care for you and will only be around while you are in a position to help them. As soon as you withdraw financial support or lose your money, the people around you will flee. Money will not ensure that your significant other loves you for who you are. In many cases, he or she is in love with the lifestyle, power, and status that comes with money.

I'm certainly not saying that having money is not beneficial. You just need to know that when you have money, people are likely to tell you what you want to hear and not the truth. Money can buy you pleasure; however, it can't buy you love. If a relationship is grounded with a foundation of love, your significant other will be there even if you suffer a health or financial setback. A relationship centered around materialism, will not withstand hardship. The third thing money cannot buy is happiness. Happiness comes from God. Money in its purest form is digits on an account. Money can buy you a lot of fun toys and experiences; however, they will not be fulfilling without healthy relationships to enjoy them with. It's important to find happiness in what you have and make the most of it. Create a financial plan, implement it, and live your life to the fullest. We can't predict the future, nor can we fathom what God has planned for us. Therefore, don't let the accumulation of money be the primary focus of your life. Because you might obtain it, but it cost you time, love, and happiness.

Chapter 12

Charity and Cheerful Giving

This is an equally important chapter of the book. Right now, I want you to reflect back on a time when someone did something nice for you, whether you were in need or not. It could have been family, friend, or stranger. I'm confident that every reader of this book can think of several instances. It could have been a financial gift, encouragement, or sage advice. Those experiences were God working through others. We have all had our own experiences with the generosity of others, which addressed a need, gave us comfort, or helped mend relationships. You may be wondering how you will know when to give to others. It's simple, listen to your conscience. It's the same inner voice that lets you know you are about to do something wrong.

Sometimes it will make sense, because you will already know the individual's need. At other times, it won't be that simple. For example, you might get a tug on your heart that you should help or donate something, or you may feel the need to share a testimony or advice to a complete stranger. Give cheerfully because you want to. Even when you are going through bad times, there are always people who have it worse than you. If you are a cheerful giver, you will not miss the things you give to others. I'm a strong believer that if you are generous, others will be generous with you. Look for opportunities to be a blessing for others by meeting their needs. There have been several times where we have donated our time, money, and clothes, because God placed us in an opportunity to be a blessing for others.

Conclusion

It's abundantly clear that many people in the middle and lower-income classes are hurting financially and/or living paycheck-to-paycheck. People have had to endure rising prices of goods and services, large medical costs, inflation, a pandemic, a public health emergency, stagnate or income reduction, and job loss. Although we are living in real tough times, we are not helpless. It's imperative that we be creative, patient, resourceful, and cheerful givers throughout our lives. It's also important to conduct your own research and listen to the advice of others. Someone may have information you don't have, which will help educate you in an area that you have limited knowledge in. However, it's equally important that you make your own decisions, based on the facts and your specific situation.

There is constant temptation encouraging us to either purchase something we don't need or need but can't afford. I recommend you use the following framework when making purchases. First, determine your needs and wants. Then, conduct research on those products and services to determine your options. Third, analyze the strengths, weaknesses, and risks of each option and determine what you are willing to pay. Lastly, consult the advice of others that are experienced in that particular area and make your final decision. When you start applying this framework, you will be amazed that you can save money and make quality purchases. A good indication of quality purchases are people contacting you with offers to buy them.

You may find that you actually couldn't afford purchases you previously made, because you lacked the knowledge of where to effectively search or research them. It's important to understand that no one knows everything. You need to be willing to listen to different points of view and experiences. I know everyone will not agree with everything in this book; however, we can agree that in life there will be times of plenty and scarcity. Therefore, you must implement prudent financial strategies that will enable you to get through the hard times. This pertains to people who earn both large and small incomes. It doesn't matter how much money you make. There are many examples of people who made millions of dollars and became broke less than a decade later.

A paradigm shift in money management is needed, because this world is not going to get easier. Now, is the time to act for you and your family's sake. It's tragic that so many people across the world work hard their whole lives, without the ability to comfortably retire and live the lifestyle that want. The solution is within reach. You just have to formulate a plan, execute the necessary adjustments in your life, and stick to it. I hope you will implement the strategies in this book, because I know for a fact they will make a positive financial impact, regardless of your situation.